The Lover's Familiar

JAMES McMICHAEL

The Lover's Familiar

DAVID R. GODINE · BOSTON

For Dozey

David R. Godine, Publisher
Boston, Massachusetts

★

Acknowledgments: The following poems first appeared
in *Poetry*: 'Lauds,' 'The Very Rich Hours,' 'Prime,'
'Terce,' 'Sext,' 'The Inland Lighthouse,' 'Nones,' 'The
Great Garret, or 100 Wheels,' 'Vespers,' and 'Its Time.'
'The Queen Anne Cottage' and 'Itinerary' first appeared
in *Antaeus*. Other poems first appeared in *Denver Quarterly*, *Hawaii Review*, and *Partisan Review*.

A Godine Poetry Chapbook
Third Series

Contents

Matins

This hour is for the lakes,
for their patience as they look through themselves,

for the light they see there,
the splinters of light
falling over their sunken ledges,
and for the patience of those ledges,

for the trees they listen for and never hear,
for the rocks,

for the cold that knows the lakes
and comes to them
and covers their clear eyes
and calms them.

Lauds

For several blocks to any
side of the schools,

sheets in the hallways
of the small houses

are laundered and stacked.
From their drawers

they send guttering
and tiny points of fire

over ivory and china,
the porcelain

basins and white tile.
Radios on the nightstands

sleep fitfully,
their dials translucent

windows to a fever.
Moths tunnel in the lawns.

A dog barks and barks.
At the curbs, the streetlamps

are unharried. Their hum
steadies to the hour.

They are everywhere
with their vague languor

as across the city
the span of each beam

rests against the next.
The shops downtown wait

absently for their Dark Night,
their glass fronts filled

with baubles and odd
trappings of their fall.

All shelves are arranged
in boredoms of clean trade.

Milk leaks a spare light
evenly through its aisle.

Below the scales in
steel bins, the almonds lie

paler than ever, sleek moons
swallowed by their own shells.

The Very Rich Hours

Amant in bed,
dreaming.
There are no
borders to this
miniature.

B moves Bateau across the night.
It is all the loops can do
to let their gilding
bulge with what is there.
One light on the wide sea.
The bones of stars.

No other country is so
curiously watered.
From the estuaries to the very
sources of its inwardtending channels,
it rises in fogs which are themselves
arterial. For its earth
has more than once been seen
quite early in the morning
to lighten and give way.

At the gate to the garden,
Fair Welcome.
She raises her hand.
Salutare:
to greet and to save.

Leisures of tendrils are on all sides,
winding with the snails

through white acanthus and discarded
badges of pilgrims.
You may assign to the nineteen
portholes in these borders
whatever you like.

The sand is of such fineness
and the flow so singly clear
that nothing seems to pass through,
golden, and with all its lights.

Water makes very much the best
portable horizon.
While its reflections are
fainter than those in the speculum,
their angles may be measured
accurately
and the differences from a true meridian
reckoned by the clock.
These sightings should be taken at least
three hours
before and after noon.

Two liveried falconers,
the jesses and bells, the gloves.
Amant with the dove's neck-ring,
the lady in her chamber.
Winter trees, rooks in the white
branches, hounds, the dying boar.
On the top of a mountain
a lion waving his tail.

The general course of the river
straightens, and is moderately timbered.
Scattered islands covered w/ willow.
Across from a single, long bluff of open rock,
the plain to the S. is higher, extending
quite to the mountains which contain still
great quantities of snow.
A small creek falls in from this side.
Pursued its bottom for perhaps 4 m.
Cottonwood. Much evidence of beaver.

Now all of this is to be understood
in a spiritual manner.
Let us cover
the nakedness of our fathers
with the cloak of a
favorable interpretation.

Under a dry stalk of burdock, iron-brown
latches and fittings, a few nails.
The bulls are eating apples.
Thick grasses sweat through the whole pasture.

Dame Reason with her
chaplet of apothegms.
He should put his heart
in a single place only.
The truest things about bodies
are their shadows.

Pleas put me back
in the water I am
Paddle-to-the-Sea

She has done this before.
She wades into the current
to the one point where the current
lounges at her hips.
She stands there.
With all the time in the world,
steadily, she kneels steadily
deeper, to her shoulders, smiling, her hair
cupped in both hands behind her neck.

The Familiar gives Its first
lesson to the lover.
A new order
is one that is renewed
hourly.

A drove of geese in its tall, white file
plucks home through the wet fallow.
Hedges darken between the fields.
Along the wolds for miles in level tracts,
haze from the lime-kilns.
All quarters of the sky are wintry, huge.

We could no longer be sure
that we had passed the Préveranges.
Freshets from the little stream
poured onto the lane, filling

13

ruts and drainages. In the dusk,
and with our shoes soaked, we set
off through a meadow, and another,
and found soon an abandoned
cottage of some old forester.
We determined that I should
stay and secure it as an outpost.
Meaulnes went on alone.

At an earlier hour,
the ground at the wood's edge
illumines to some thousand
footcandles, fades under the
canopies, the layers
of trees, of shrubs and herbs,
under the dark itself,
brighter by as many
eyes as are buried there.

Tied to a washboard,
submerged,
the panes of glass
chime like clean ice.

they are dangers harebells and
just where the fall goes over
they lean into the spray so
far and bob so on their stems
they thrill and a hammer rings
carillon down the cows spine
feel it there it goes again

14

Death hath its seat
close to the entrance of delight.
            —Gudique

Sifting over porches and limp hibiscus,
rust from the canvas awnings,
its red spores dull in a moon that shows
everything, houses and driveways,
fishponds, all of them
hiding from their insides, forgetting,
looking around.

    there is no way to lie down
    and not lie in the same way
    that someone has had to lie
    thinking of how far it is
    to the places no one goes
    or to any place this far
    from the beds where the dying
    cry into the night this far

Deacons and presbyters.
The Laying On of Hands.
In a vial,
juice from the wild cucumber,
powdered glass,
the divine Endura.

Prime

Towers look across
to other
towers and to tall stores.
They look to the mountains
which are their help.

The sky comes down
weightlessly
into these
spaces the town leaves.

With the lonely
grace of what it fills
it comes down

weightlessly
and is all of it,

is the sky coming there.

Terce

Between the walls, the brim
between the air and the water
fits, presses where it can into

corners, into cracks that freeze.
With its pressing into their sighs
it spares the walls

nothing, sends them for breath
into their own pains,
into what they remember about being

one stone, breathing, the brim
away somewhere, not pressing.
As it slips through their dark course

the seams that once bound them
narrow and clutch, shudder to take
more, to take enough,

coming and coming to be so close.
The brim curls at its edges, lapping.
The air and the water go their ways.

Lutra, the Fisher

The otter is known
for the way his face turns up
anywhere.

On silver coins
or from behind mahogany bureaus

he wears the aspect of a suckling,
innocent
and helplessly

shocked that he should be caught so,

napkin under chin,
his dinner folded
head to tail between his jaws
like a limp bow.

When he goes to work

the surprise is
that he is there at all.

His long neck of a body
streams like sunken
weed-strands,

rises and trails the quiet wake
of any log or stone.

Even in the shallows

he is the thought of his own
absence
and can be found at home

as water would be found there,

filling the den
or strewing over the kitchen floor

bones and vermillion gills.

Itinerary

The farmhouses north of Driggs,
silos for miles along the road saying
BUTLER or SIOUX. The light saying
rain coming on, the wind not up yet,
animals waiting as the front hits
everything on the high flats, hailstones
bouncing like rabbits under the sage.
Nothing running off. Creeks clear.
The river itself a shallow, straight
shoot to the north, its rocks mossy,
slick above the few deep pockets.
On another drainage, the O-T-O.
Loose stands of aspen on the slopes.
Dude cabins, their porches and split-log
loveseats, dull yellow curtains
slapping over the open sills.
From Emigrant north to the Great Bend,
loaves of haystacks, stud farms, charolais,
steel flumes between the ditches.
Access to the river's acreage
closed to its whole length, the county roads
dusty, turning onto the high
shelves of side valleys. Scattered
shacks and corrals. An old homestead,
the sod roof rotting out its timbers.
Below the spurs from the higher range,
basins in the mountain pastures
fill with odd water. The henbane dries.
Ruts cross in the grass at a schoolhouse.
Each runnel mixing where it can
the spring creeks deepen and go on

easily, swelling to the larger
tributary with its pools and banks.
At any bend the willows bend too,
and gravel bars on the other shore
flare into the shallows. An encampment.
Ponies wade to their knees and drink,
raising up now and then to look
out through the smoke to the near hills,
the one plateau heading off beyond
the Crazies and the Little Belts, north.
It strikes the river at the Gates,
the water piling through its broad course,
level, ridges and the vertical
faces of bluffs crowding to each side.
This rock is of an excellent grit for
whetstones, hard and sharp. There is here
more timber than below the falls. A spring
immensely clear and of a bluish cast
boils up near its center with such force
that its surface in that part is strangely
higher than the surrounding earth.
I heard today a noise resembling
the discharge of a piece of ordnance.
Unless it be the bursting of the
rich mines of silver in these mountains,
I am at a loss to account for it.
As the passages about the falls are
narrow and steep, and as the buffalo
travel to the river in great herds,
the hinder part presses those in front
out of their depth to the strong current.

Their carcasses by the hundreds
litter the shore below the cataracts.
We have made of the mast of the pirogue
two axletrees. Walked ahead to my first
view of the falls, hearing them from afar.
Their spray is scarcely formed when
bodies of the same beaten water thrust
over and down, concealing every shape,
their whiteness alone visible.
We will leave at this place all heavy
baggage, the red pirogue, and whatever
provisions we can do without. Needing
a cellar for the caching of our stores
we set hands to digging. More white bear.
These fellows leave a formidable
impression in the mud or sand. Goodrich,
who is remarkably fond of fishing,
caught many trout of two different species.
Came to in a handsome timbered bottom
across from the entrance of a very
considerable river. Its character
is so precisely that of the one below
that the party with few exceptions
has pronounced it the Missouri.
The fork to the south is perfectly
transparent, runs rapidly with an even,
unriffled surface. Its bed is composed
of round, smooth stones like those of rivers
issuing from a mountainous country.
If this latter be the one we are to take
we should encounter within 50 miles

a series of precipitous falls.
There is now no timber on the hills.
The black rock has given place to a
yellow and brown or black clay, brown and
yellowish white sandstone and a hard, dark
freestone. It rises from the water
abruptly on both sides in varied walls.
I could discover above their horizon
only the most elevated points.
The river retains both its whitish color
and a proportion of its sediment,
but it is much clearer than below.
The banks afforded us good towing.
This method of ascending the river
is the safest and most expeditious.
We pass a great number of dry streambeds.
These plains being level and wholly
destitute of timber, the wind blows
violently with its loads of sand.
Driftwood comes down as the water rises.
The banks are falling in very fast
and I wonder that our pirogues are not
swallowed by them. Wild hyssop grows here.
A few cottonwood along the verges.
Undergrowths of rose and serviceberry,
and small-leafed willow on the sandbars.
Met this evening the famous white bear.
I had rather deal with several
indians than with this gentleman.
Much less ice running in the river.
We make ready to set out, the party

in general good health except for a few
venereal complaints. A windy,
blustering day. Our two pirogues still frozen.
I draw a connection of the country
from the information of traders.
The falls are about 800 miles west.
Rose early and commenced roofing
the two wings of huts. Our situation
sandy. Cottonwood and elm, some small ash.
We must now settle for the winter.
Very cold. Hard frosts. The river falling.
For several days we pass deserted
Mandan villages along both banks.
The beaver and otter are becoming more
abundant. We put ashore at noon,
setting fire to the prairies to signal
that we wish council with the natives.
These Arikara much reduced by pox.
It is customary for their nation
to show its grief by pain, some cutting off
two smaller fingers at the second joint.
The earth of the plains is in many places
opened in long crevices, its soil
indifferent and with a kind of timothy
branching like flax from its main stalk.
Delayed here today so as to take
equal altitudes, the weights of the
waters of the two rivers, their specific
gravities. As we near the great Platte,
the sandbars are more numerous, sawyers
worse than they were below. Mulberry,

oak and walnut. These prairies from the river
have very much the appearance of farms.
We continue to pole our way upstream.
Notwithstanding our precautions, we
struck a bar and were near turning over.
The sergeants are directed each to keep
a journal of all passing occurrences
and such other descriptions of the country
as shall seem to them worthy of notice.
Our hunters report deer in every copse.
I got out and walked for one mile through a
rush bottom, nettles as high as my breast.
All the forepart of the day we were
arranging our company and taking on
those articles we will need. St. Charles.
The men spent their last night agreeably,
dancing with the French ladies, &c.
My ride was on a road finely shaded,
with now and then a good farm. The corn
in tassel, its leaves of a deep rich green
bending at the ends by their own weight.
Wheat and oat stubble. A hilly country.
I passed a toll-gate, and, looking back,
had my last view of the town's steeples.
From the state house cupola I could count
the buildings, the number of which was
ninety. A wooden bridge crosses the river
just below the town. Men were engaged in
racing their horses. I sought lodging
and was shown to bed in a large barrack
where a man and wife conversed with me

until I feigned sleep. This is a post town,
the mails arriving from both east and west
on Wednesdays and Saturdays. A young woman
gave me directions from an upstairs window.
I descended the hill into Frankfort.
There has lately been established a large
manufactory for spinning hemp and flax.
It is wrought by water and keeps in motion
1200 spindles. The streets of Lexington
cross at right angles, its stores filled both
with imports and with local goods: fine
cutlery, tin ware, muslins and nankeens.
I was so well put up that a man would be
fastidious to a fault to have found
the least thing wanting. Approaching the city
the land changed steadily for the better,
no longer broken, as to the eastward,
but fine extensive levels and slopes,
the road very wide, with grazing parks,
meadows, and every spot cultivated.
The farms hereabout have generally
good and spacious stone barns, a few acres
cleared but for those stumps or girdled trees
still standing. The neighbors found last year
a human jawbone, rough and honeycombed.
My wagoner arrived this afternoon
and went on, appointing to be in
Louisville before me. I pass a house
with small turrets at its corners, lawns,
the whole needing only vineyards for the look
of villas in Provence and Languedoc.

Noticed along the banks of the Holston
phlox with white flowers and phlox with pink flowers,
two different species, very small
phlox with lance-shaped leaves. Where I
come in from Abingdon, the Kentucky road
divides, the other fork for Burke courthouse.
With nothing to do I make ink from gall nuts.
More opossum taken in the woods.
This animal's greatest peculiarity
is the false belly of the female.
She can draw the slit so close that one must look
narrowly to find it if she be virgin.
The air clearing this morning, I was
surprised with a full prospect of mountains.
This river where we leave off is 240 miles
distant in a straight line from Currituck
Inlet. The turkey-cocks begin to gobble,
which is the language wherein they make love.
We have a dreamer of dreams among us
who warned me in the morning to take care
that I not fall into the creek.
I thanked him and used what caution I could,
but my horse made a false leap and laid me
down in the water at my full length.
The sky at sunset had a swept look.
There was risk of our dining with St. Anthony
when one indian knocked down a fat bear.
Of the stem of the silk-grass their women make
small aprons which they wear for decency.
They put these on with so much art
that their most negligent postures reveal

nothing to our curiosity.
The ruffles of some of our fellows
were a little discolored by the bloodroot
which these ladies use to improve their charms.
Bear, it would seem, is no diet for saints,
for it is apt to make them too rampant.
At night, the surveyors took advantage
of a clear sky. This trial of our variance
shows it still something less than 3 degrees,
so it remains much as we had found it
at the sea. We have now run the poles
beyond those inhabitants most inland.
There fell a sort of Scots mist all the way.
I have learned how rattlesnakes take a squirrel.
They ogle the poor beast till by force of charm
it falls down stupefied and senseless.
The snake approaches it and moistens first
one ear and then the other with his spittle,
making the head all slippery. When that is done
he draws this member into his mouth,
and after it, by casual degrees,
all the rest of the body. I am not so
rigid an observer of the Sabbath
as to allow of no journeys to be
taken upon it. Nor would I care,
like a certain New England magistrate,
to order a man to the whipping post
for daring to ride for a midwife on the
Lord's Day. And yet we found plainly
that travelling on the Sunday had not
thriven with us in the least. The rain

was enlivened with loud thunder, and there is
something in the woods that makes this sound
more awful, the violence of the lightning
more visible as the trees are shivered
quite to the root. This Great Dismal Swamp
is the source of five several rivers.
We run our line to its skirts, which begin with
dwarf reeds, moist uneven ground. The season
inclining us to aguish distempers,
we were suffered by the resident to
cut up wood for firing, drive away the damps.
At the bottom of the account Mankind
are great losers by the luxuries
of feather beds and warm apartments.
We perceive our appetites to mend,
and though we have to drink only what
Adam had in Paradise, that stream of life
runs cool and peaceably in our veins.
The days are hard. Our slumbers sweeten, and
if ever we dream of women they are kind.
I delight to see the banks of the Inlet
adorned with myrtle, yet it must be owned
that, sacred to Venus though it be, this plant
grows commonly in very dirty soil.
Norfolk has most the air of a town
of any in Virginia. There are now
riding at her wharves near 20 brigantines.
The trade hither is engrossed by those
saints of New England who every week
carry off a pretty deal of tobacco.
I have found that after my devotions

a walk in the garden can do much
to fill my heart with clear obedience.
I repair me there that I might think
deeply of the earth and how it will be
all too soon my sleeping-place. For I am told
to fear such things as bring me to ill terms,
told of those who seek congress with the earth
that they shall have her in their time forever.
That her places sing their love-songs for no man.
That I am not the suitor whose betrothed
awaits him, but some unwelcome third
with God alone her lover. And yet I would
look upon such country as will show me
nature undressed, the strata of the land,
her lays and beds and all her privacies.
For my wonder tells me I should be
promiscuous, should learn by all the
laws of bodies and by where they are
the joyful news out of the new found world.
This walk is news. Its bodies point me always
in and out along some newer course.
There have been divers days together
wherein alone I've watched these flowers
buoyed on their stems and holding up the sun.
Just now I catch them thinking on themselves,
composing from their dark places the least
passages for light, tendering how they look
and how I look on them. It comes to me
that the world is to the end of it
thinking on itself and how its parts
gather with one another for their time.

These are the light, and all the forms they show
are lords of inns wherein the soul takes rest.
If I could find it in myself to hide
the world within the world then there would be
no place to which I could remove it, save
that brightness wherein all things come to see.

Sext

The air binds in sockets
around its few trees,
their arms crazed and spiny.
Tailing from the loose floor
shines where the sky holds it.
For as far as it carries,

the Dead Heart takes its hour
deliberately, this full light
scraping through its washes
and over the tired outcrop,
missing nothing, rooting in all
fissures, wearing it down.

The Inland Lighthouse

Into the night,
out from him,
out into the air
he throws his frames
and fixes them,
holds them out there.

These are his shores.
The waters never
rush at him, never
follow the beams
back along the watch
to his lean shiver.

Around him, as he
turns, he hears
a dull tick of grains.
He stares into the day.
Sand fills the sky
with its falling

and he turns and turns.
'Nowhere. Nowhere.'
It is his oath.
He is the light,
the keeper.
He is not to leave.

Nones

The day has found next door another
roofline tiles next door again some shade
prim clotheslines furniture the chalky

stucco of garages haze and trellised
carports driveways gravels fills of brick
old angles down the inclines where the

grey and scored warm plates of sidewalk
level with the aprons there is more
somewhere than these streets their careful yards

The Great Garret, or 100 Wheels

The curricle and hansom
pretend to such size as would send them

shaking along the lanes
and past the gates to closes,

their separate pedigrees lettered
neatly on each undercarriage: 'H. R.

Waiting' and 'Thos. 1775 Beeton.'
They huddle among the rafters with

models of sedans, wains, herring carts,
cabriolets and a barouche,

all kept at rest in some autistic
pageant of transport, or by the staid

example of the wind toy, its soldiers
frozen forever in mid-stride.

Only the cycles have a muscular past.
From the treadles of the *Draisienne*

it is as far to any point on the whole
vast chase of the manor

as to the next of the measured
interstices between the spokes.

Turning is what would change this.
Because they never turn,

the niceties of the garden are clearly
here, nearer the pediments than those

outlying, lesser strips of arable.
Clearly the forecourts are not behind.

Predictably, and with perfect rigor,
they front for the house in its fixed

severance from the village and the fields.
Because they never turn,

landmarks of this and that are where they are.
Wooded hollows and the Windrush.

Stray brakes of hawthorn on the slopes.
Sheepwalks. Trails. Uncertain rights of drift.

The Queen Anne Cottage

The paths are dutiful.
They swell up only as the contours
call upon them for help.

At slight rises
or where a tree has repressed too much

they are at ease.

Sometimes they cross one another
and go off toward so many enclosures that they startle

even the novelist.
They evade her like poachers
just as she is placing her mansion behind the firs.
She is left supposing they entered the garden
here or maybe
here

and the clouds cannot wait for her
and the dusk loses its memory and shines
and the old berlin draws up in front of the wrong gate.

Or they may pass as roads.

The horizon can seldom tell
if they are coming or going.
They make it turn itself out into the distance
again and again.

The Queen Anne knows
that this is what the paths have to do.
She likes their seriousness

how they address the steps
with no hesitation take them
boldly and steadily at perfect
angles onto her veranda floor.

She thinks they are the boards of this floor.
They have no trouble staying down.
The nails are not so much
holding them
as wanting their heads to find
a good level place.

If she is the paths
they do not come into her at each side
as she does not go out.

Everything turns so
on where she might be said to be.

If she is the paths
and trembles with a light fine
palsy through the whole
Valley of the Sweetest Name of Jesus of the Earthquakes

the dust that rises with the shaking
covers her secret flanks

tight draws
where foxes slant through yucca on steep
switchbacks to the crests.

If she coos to the hills to play
Touch Me Here
and
Honor Thy Creases

if she calls them her Dove her Supper

they quit their prayers
for steadfastness their

meditations on the ease of plains and on the
holiness of vast distresses of boredom they
breathe her as if their being
expires where she
leaves off.

If she is breathed
she is no longer in the delirium of seven
hardships the hardship of

triangulation the hardship of
Great Bandy Leg Walk the hardship of
construe the hardship of
summer sketching tours the hardship of
porte-cochère the hardship of
it is not permitted the hardship of
doctor doll with skull on its foot.

Her walls give over their absurd disguises
if she is where the paths stop.

Yes when they are called upon to lie down
as she herself feels called upon
to lie down

her walls give over their absurd disguises.
If she is where the paths stop

her gambrels and dormers and spindles
and ramped rails
give over their disguises and she is left with
everything she can see.

There is sweet alyssum for eyes.
Its flakes of petals are the presence of all color.
It is on its way out into the world.
The benches take it on they need it.
Without it the palms are forgotten and workaday.
The mud can wait forever but it goes there too.
At the reeds and bamboo flutes

it slides with the frogs into the pond.
It is amazed.

Here is the sky insisting adamant letting

nothing have its way nothing no not the
lilies trying to hold it off nor the carp coming
up through the tight blue

membrane no nor night nor that obscene fruit
the moon.

The sky is as secure within the pond's shores
as in the hollow of its own hand.

It tenders the Queen's profile.
Cupola.
Bracketed roofs
and thicktongued scrollsaws.
Baskets of fuchsia hanging from the eaves in
ponderous drooping scrota.
White straight chaste colonnades.

From the heart of the pond
the sky tells the simple happiness
of spilling over weirs
evenly
as with an eye to glass.

It tells of the blue
turrets of Azay-le-Rideau
rising like a surprise from intricate
watercourses.

It goes on and on
and tells that she herself is
the River Stour grazing through fields

flat

her eddies
whispering around stumps of old bridges
that she will not be back.

For below a single
hay wain crossing at the ford

below the mill

dense oaks are waiting to be spelled.
Their sequestering has brought them to this.
In their cells along both banks

the river is their solace from far places
their window

and as they draw from her

their higher branches
open with a faint gold to lower
clusters of oak

to the gold of the fields

the sky

to the dark rich
amplitude of the far clouds moving on.

Vespers

They were taking back
against themselves to their first springs
the evening and its light.
They could be sure of wells,
had lined those holes with the cool
liverworts of upland coverts.

Their readiness was in what they knew
of doorsteps and of worn stone bridges,
how they had drawn around them to the broader
millflats, slowing, the cattle bending
quietly to their own tongues.
There was the dry-dock baggage:

ladles and cauldrons, ribs,
new barges waiting on their timbers.
All shows of trees,
the open looks between them to the hills—
they would take these back and cleanse them,
they had been their widest there.

Its Time

Conserved in dews.
Yellows. The yellow

distillates of white.
How the heat in its

mean free path fills
inch by inch the blue

middle distance,
each plank and leaf

deeper by each plane,
each body saving

place in the late
morning. Squat barges

adrift along the
towpath. Beams of locks.

The canal, its calm
glazed heart bending

inland, further,
between the fields,

a seam in their deep
brightness, saving up.

How change is saved
in strong parities—

for the grasses, the
light of any hour,

grasses for what light
the clouds let through

over Homestalls,
Mithers and Trims' Green.

Stores of it in jars:
from the Common,

mosses and lichens,
barks, her colored soils,

the umber, pleated
furnaces of dank

mushrooms. Its true darks
lost under varnish

of violins,
of cart grease, tar

or snuff of candles.
That its time on all

surfaces is change;
that these accidents,

45

its meetings, redden
through interiors

in flares and rich
traces of its source;

that its colors and
colored lights and shades

withdraw around the
leaded mullions,

its low angles
framed against the walls,

changing, each canvas
sure of what it holds;

that it lasts this long
is light's strangeness.

Compline

Gudique is the chastening.
She is not a fish.

She is not the rocks where she browses
nor the pools.

The river when it opens
is not Gudique.

When its forgetfulness
falls from it,

when a cold wind leaks
upward through the drifts and folds and

pours over the banks
and over the ferns

this is not Gudique.
Gudique is the chastening,

the river forgetting
Gudique is the river.

DATE DUE